Sperm whale

Humpback whale

WHALE FALL
CAFÉ

Written by
Jacquie Sewell

Illustrated by
Dan Tavis

TILBURY HOUSE PUBLISHERS,
THOMASTON, MAINE

The bottom of the ocean is

DEEP

DARK

and

COLD.

There's life down there,
but animals need special
adaptations to withstand the
enormous water pressure of the
deep ocean. Although I am a fish,
I'd die instantly in water that
deep. Why do you think I'm in
this **SUBMERSIBLE***?

(By the way, * marks a word
that's defined in the Glossary.)

Extraordinary creatures live
in the deepest parts of the ocean.

Some of them **GLOW** in the dark.

Some of them have **HUGE** eyes.

Some of them have
Transparent
heads.

And some of them live on **WHALE FALLS.**

I must be really hungry, because that submarine looks delicious.

I can hear you thinking, Wait! What is a whale fall?

I'm so glad you asked!

A whale fall is the carcass of a whale on the deep ocean floor.

Humpback whale

Orca (killer whale)

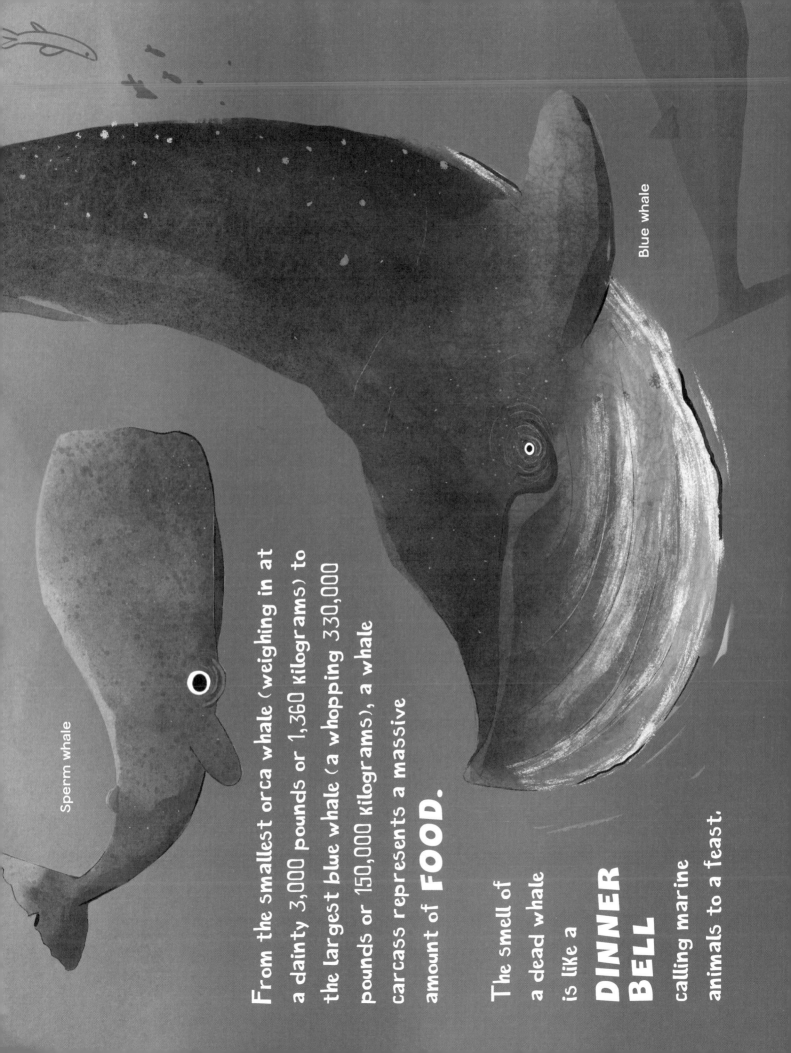

Blue whale

Sperm whale

From the smallest orca whale (weighing in at a dainty 3,000 pounds or 1,360 kilograms) to the largest blue whale (a whopping 330,000 pounds or 150,000 kilograms), a whale carcass represents a massive amount of **FOOD.**

The smell of a dead whale is like a

DINNER BELL

calling marine animals to a feast.

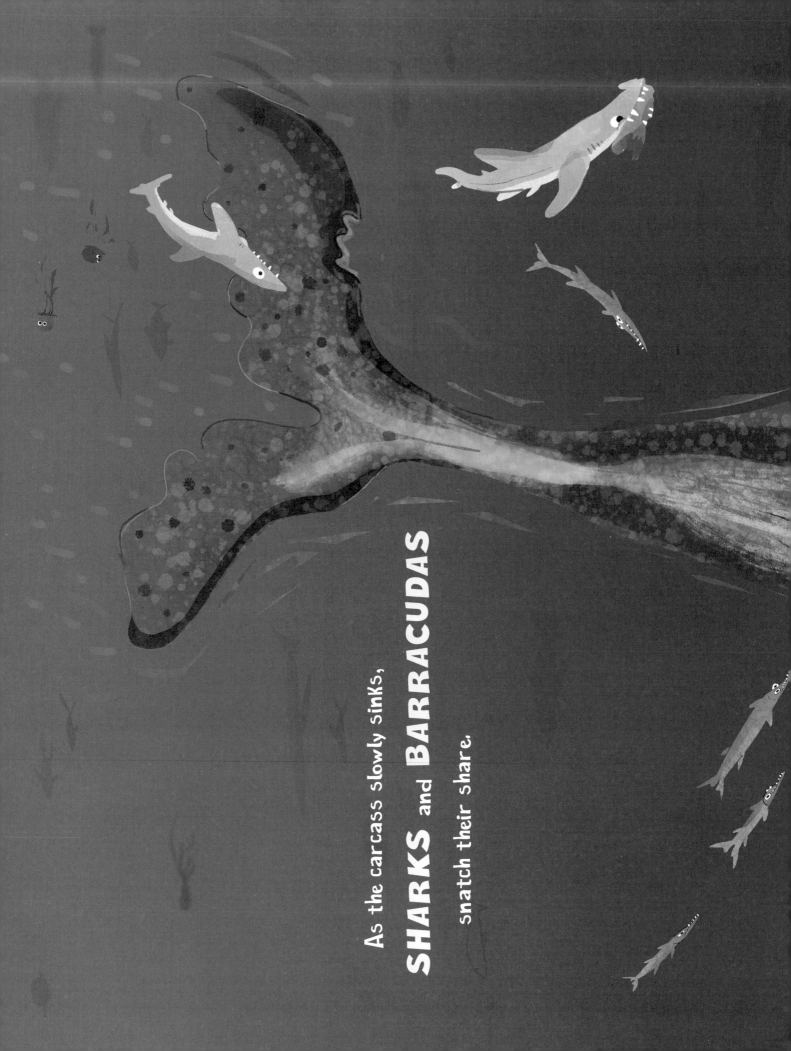

As the carcass slowly sinks,

SHARKS and **BARRACUDAS**

snatch their share.

These animals usually eat **MARINE SNOW***, animal bits and waste that drift down (like snowflakes) from the water above. One medium-size whale (say, 44 tons or 40,000 kilograms) provides as much food as 4,000 years of marine snow. Now that's a **BONANZA***!

The minute the
WHALE FALL CAFÉ
opens, hagfish
are on their way.

These mobile
SCAVENGERS*
have a keen sense
of smell that
makes up for their
lack of sight.

SLEEPER SHARKS
aren't far behind.

These

PROFICIENT PREDATORS

love a free meal. They tear off huge chunks of flesh with their powerful jaws.

Other scavengers joining the feast include rattails, an assortment of crabs and crustaceans, and roly-polies (giant isopods) bigger than **HOUSE CATS.**

Once the mobile scavengers have finished, all that is left is the
SKELETON.

End of story, you're thinking—but wait!

The second seating at the Whale Fall Café features an even more **BIZARRE** group of diners . . .

. . . like zombie worms, which are also called bone-eating snot worms. These **SPECIALISTS***thrive on whale falls and were first discovered in 2002.

Scientists call them *Osedax**.

They have no mouth or gut, but they do have long, root-like structures that bore into whale bone and anchor them to the whale fall. Bacteria inside these "roots" break down fats and proteins in the bones, making food for the worm.

Waiting their turn at the whale fall bonanza is another group of bacteria with a special superpower. They don't need sunlight to survive!

Which is good, because, remember, the bottom of the ocean is deep, dark, and cold. No sunlight down there! Plants can't live on the deepest ocean floor, but

CHEMOAUTOTROPHIC BACTERIA* can!

Also called **EXTREMOPHILES**, chemoautotrophic bacteria are the first link in a unique food chain. They live in a variety of clams, mussels, and seaworms found on whale falls, and they convert hydrogen sulfide (produced by their fellow diners) into carbohydrates, thus providing food for their hosts.

This last **SEATING** at the
Whale Fall Café can go on for years.

Now that was a whale of a meal.

The worms, bacteria, and
their crustacean friends feast
away until every edible bit of
the whale has been chomped,
chewed, dissolved and devoured.

When the last morsel of nutrition is consumed, it's

LIGHTS OUT

at the Whale Fall Café.

Or is it?

A whale fall is a **GIFT** that Keeps on **GIVING.**

Stripped clean and hollowed out, its bones provide support for corals, sea lilies and other creatures that live in colonies on the ocean floor.

Thousand-year-old whale bones have been found encrusted with **ANEMONES**.

Whales can live **100 YEARS** in the wild.

In their death they provide life and a habitat for thousands of creatures, for **CENTURIES**.

GLOSSARY

Anemone: soft-bodied, brightly colored marine animal that resembles a flower because of its ring of tentacles

Benthic: the benthic zone is the lowest level of a body of water

Bonanza: a sudden increase of something desirable

Chemoautotrophic bacteria: bacteria that generate energy from inorganic sources, like hydrogen sulfide on a whale fall

Extremophiles: organisms that live in inhospitable environments, like whale falls or deep-sea vents (hot spots on the ocean floor created by seawater superheated by the earth's magma)

Marine snow: tiny bits of dead algae and dead sea creatures (and their waste)

Osedax: Latin for "bone-eating"

Scavenger: an animal that feeds on dead animals and plants and refuse

Specialists: species that can thrive only in a narrow range of environmental conditions

Submersible: a small submarine that allows travel through the deep, dark and cold ocean depths

GOING DEEPER

Barreleye: The Fish with a Transparent Head

Barreleye fish have tubular, telescoping eyes that allow them to see in the dim light of the deep ocean. A transparent, fluid-filled dome covers their eyes. Scientists speculate that this protective dome allows the barreleye to steal food from deep-sea jellies (called Siphonophores) without being injured by their stinging tentacles. Barreleyes—about 8 inches (20 cm) long—have large, flat fins that propel them through the water with precision or maintain their position, motionless, while they wait for prey.

Hagfish

Hagfish range in length from 18 to 32 inches (46 - 81 cm). They have no scales, no fins, and no bones, but they do have mucus glands—lots of them. When provoked, a hagfish secretes copious amounts of mucus from the 100 glands lining

each side of its body. The viscous slime swells in seawater, enveloping the hagfish in a protective cocoon of goo. To avoid drowning in its own mucus, a hagfish can tie itself in a knot and pass its body through the knot, pulling the slime off as it goes.

Its lack of jaws for munching doesn't stop a hagfish from enjoying a free meal. It uses four rows of teeth on a protractible cartilaginous plate to burrow into the whale carcass and devour the decaying flesh.

Sleeper Sharks

Sleeper sharks were once thought to be sluggish denizens of the deep, but research has proven just the opposite. They swim continuously, zigging and zagging up and down through the water in

an oscillating pattern. In one study, a sleeper shark traveled 12,000 vertical meters (more than 7 vertical miles) in a 24-hour period. Perhaps they should be called Sleepless Sharks!

Sleeper sharks glide noiselessly through the water with little body movement, sneaking up on their prey in stealth mode. With a sudden burst of speed from its broad tailfin, this silent hunter has the advantage when chasing seals, salmon, or other "fast foods."

Oversized olfactory bulbs in their brain alert sleeper sharks to the smell of a decaying whale, and they are quick to join the chow wagon. Using their strong jaws, they peel off and devour strips of blubber from the carcass, then gorge on the muscle beneath. Almost every sleeper shark caught by fishermen has whale flesh in its belly.

Rattails

Rattails (grenadier fish) are brown, silver, or black benthic fish. (Benthic fish live on or just above the seafloor.) Rattails have large heads, huge eyes, and a wide mouth, but it's their long, slender tails that earn them their nickname.

 They are among the most common deep-sea fish, making an appearance at every submersible dive spot, shipwreck, and underwater land-mark. Most are of moderate size, less than 3 feet (1 meter) long.

Rattails' acute hearing and sense of smell help them locate food in the inky depths of the ocean. They are not fussy about what they eat. In addition to whale falls, they will dine on other fish, crustaceans (such as shrimp), and cephalopods (such as squid and octopus).

Isopods

Next time you turn over a rock, pick up one of the roly-poly bugs that try to scurry away. Ro-ly-poly bugs, or pill bugs, are land-living crustaceans called isopods. Look closely at the little

 creature and try to imagine it 25 times that size! *Bathynomus giganteus*, roly-poly's deep-sea cousin, can grow that big—up to two-and-a-half feet (76 cm) in length. This rather freakishly large scavenger is another frequent diner at whale falls. Scientists have several theories for why *B. giganteus* grows so big. Per-

haps the cold temperatures on the ocean floor help them live longer and grow bigger cells. Whatever the reason, there's no doubt that this is one roly-poly you'd rather not find in your rock pile.

Osedax

When scientists first studied *Osedax* worms, they were surprised that all the specimens were female. Further research by Dr. Greg Rouse of Scripps Institution of Oceanography revealed the

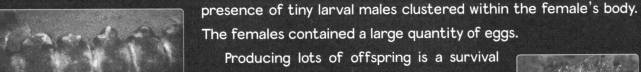 presence of tiny larval males clustered within the female's body. The females contained a large quantity of eggs.

Producing lots of offspring is a survival tactic for *Osedax*. Because they live exclu-sively on bones, they die once the skeleton's

lipids have been consumed. To ensure their species' continuation, *Osedax* worms release massive quantities of eggs into the ocean currents so that

some will survive—"just like a dandelion," says Dr. Robert Vrijenhoek, a researcher at the Mon-terey Bay Aquarium Research Institute.

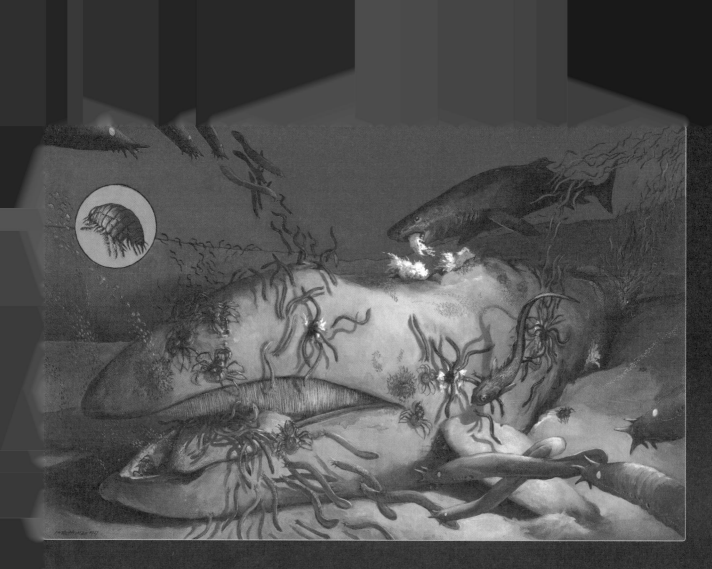

No one had ever seen a dead whale on the bottom of the ocean until 1987. That's when students from the University of Hawaii, while surveying the ocean floor in a submersible, spotted a pile of bones—dinosaur bones, they thought! But Dr. Craig

Smith, head of the research team, knew at a glance they weren't dinosaur bones. They were whale bones, probably from a blue whale, the largest creature on earth. A blue whale can grow as big as a jet and weigh more than 400,000 pounds (180,000 kg). Its tongue alone weighs as much as an elephant!

You're probably wondering: If whales are so big, why hadn't anyone ever found a dead one on the ocean floor before? Well, the ocean is huge. It covers almost 140 million square miles (362 million square kilometers)—more than 70% of the earth's surface—and it's deep, dark, and cold. So finding a dead whale—a *whale fall*, as scientists call them—is like finding a speck of dust on the beach.

Since natural whale falls are so hard to find, scientists create their own to study.

Don't worry—they don't kill any whales. When a whale carcass washes up on a beach, scientists race to get there before it decomposes. Then they tow it out to sea, weight it down with iron train wheels and heavy chains, mark the location where it sinks, and go home and burn their clothes. (According to Dr. Smith, dead whales smell pretty putrid.)

Having their own whale fall is a huge help to scientists like Dr. Smith. It allows them to keep tabs on the carcass and see who's coming to dinner, because that's

what a whale fall is—a huge banquet for creatures that live in the dark, cold ocean depths. Scientists have recorded more than 175 species of deep-sea animals feasting on whale falls.

Dr. Smith's discovery in 1987 opened an exciting field of scientific research. New species are discovered on whale falls almost daily, many with secrets still to be discovered. Each species plays a role in Earth's circle of life, from the great whale that supports diverse life for decades after its death, to the smallest bacterium that fuels a complex food web.

The Whale Fall Café would be a far less interesting book without the contributions of Dr. Craig Smith, Dr. Robert Vrijenhoek, and the Monterey Bay Aquarium Research Institute.

Dr. Craig Smith is a Professor of Oceanography at the University of Hawaii. His research focuses on the ecology of habitats in the deepest parts of the ocean. Dr. Smith's love of the ocean and its inhabitants began when he was five years old. His family lived on a sailboat for two years sailing the Adriatic Sea. He still spends much of his time on the water. As an oceanographer, Smith's research has taken him from the abyssal plains (the deep-sea floor) to the frigid waters of Antarctica. He studies the unique ecosystems that thrive in such extreme environments and the impact of changing temperatures on these fragile systems.

Imagine discovering an animal no one had ever seen before. For **Dr. Robert Vrijenhoek**, that was one of the most exciting aspects of his work at the Monterey Bay Aquarium Research Institute in California.

During his career as an evolutionary biologist, Dr. Vrijenhoek led deep-sea expeditions around the world studying, and discovering, new species of crabs, clams, mussels, snails, and worms. "We learn from the uncommon," says Dr. Vrijenhoek. "Such things tell us a little bit more about what is normal. Studying extreme examples defines the limits to life on this planet and opens our eyes to possibilities elsewhere."

At heart, Dr. Vrijenhoek is still a nine-year-old boy who likes to play in mud puddles. He describes being a scientist like living in Neverland. "Creative scientists don't have to grow up. They find rewards in looking at the world with a childlike wonder, asking endless questions about how things work, how things came to be, why things work one way rather than some other way, and not being easily satisfied with answers found in the textbooks."

And sometimes they get to name the cool creatures they discover after their friends and colleagues, or have one named after themselves!

Monterey Bay Aquarium Research Institute in Moss Landing, California.

The Monterey Bay Aquarium Research Institute (MBARI) was founded in 1987 by David Packard, who believed the ocean is "the most important frontier we have left." MBARI is committed to a unique partnership of science and engineering for the purpose of exploring and understanding the ocean—from the smallest atom to the most remote ecosystem. MBARI researchers work together to advance sustainable marine resource management and help the public understand the ocean's importance to our daily lives.

Text © 2021 by Jacquie Sewell
Illustrations © 2021 by Dan Tavis

Hardcover ISBN 978-0-88448-848-4

Tilbury House Publishers • Thomaston, Maine • www.tilburyhouse.com

Library of Congress Control Number: 2020951872

Designed by Frame25 Productions • Printed in Korea

10 9 8 7 6 5 4 3 2 1

Jacquie Sewell is a former children's librarian and the author of *Mighty Mac: The Bridge That Michigan Built*. She honed her history and science writing skills as a freelance writer for *Lansing City Limits Magazine*, hospital publications, *Cobblestone Magazine*, and others. Visit her at www.jacquiesewell.com.

Dan Tavis has been doodling since his first math class in elementary school. He is the illustrator of *Common Critters* (Tilbury House, 2020) and indulges his passion to illustrate characters that emotionally connect with the viewer and tell stories through a visual narrative. Dan creates illustrations with watercolor, ink, and digital media. Visit him at dantavis.com.

BACKMATTER IMAGES: CAPTIONS AND CREDITS

Going Deeper

Barreleye fish: Monterey Bay Aquarium Research Institute • *Hagfish* (left): Paulo Oliveira/Alamy • *Hagfish* (right): Mark Conlin/Alamy • *Sleeper sharks*: Monterey Bay Aquarium Research Institute • *Rattails* (left): Monterey Bay Aquarium Research Institute • *Rattails* (right): Monterey Bay Aquarium Research Institute • *Isopods* (left): Linda Zelnio/iStock • *Isopods* (right): Aquarium of the Pacific • *Osedax worms on whale vertebrae* (left): Monterey Bay Aquarium Research Institute • *Osedax worms on whale bone* (right): Monterey Bay Aquarium Research Institute.

The Discovery of a Whale Fall

Illustration of a fresh whale fall is by Michael Rothman • Photo of scavengers on a 30-ton gray whale carcass is by Craig Smith • Photo of a deep-sea red crab (there are several species) is by Craig Smith • Photo of a six-year-old whale fall covered with chemoautotrophic bacteria is by Craig Smith.

In their explorations, scientists from MBARI often encounter creatures they've never seen before. Meet some of their favorites at: *www.mbari.org/products/creature-feature/*

Monterey Bay Aquarium also offers online courses in the marine sciences. Take a trip to the deep sea, study otters up close, and more! Enroll for free at: *www.montereybayaquarium.org/for-educators/learning-at-home/online-courses*

In October 2019, a team from the *Nautilus* Exploration Program discovered a whale fall while exploring the Davidson Seamount off California's coast. They filmed their discovery so you can share their excitement as they zoom in on rattails, hagfish, and octopuses feasting on a whale fall. See: *www.youtube.com/watch?v=CZzQhiNQXxU&list=PLzWqlRil3fGdNpZz1ek0k9Vatmpzoin Ma&index=5*

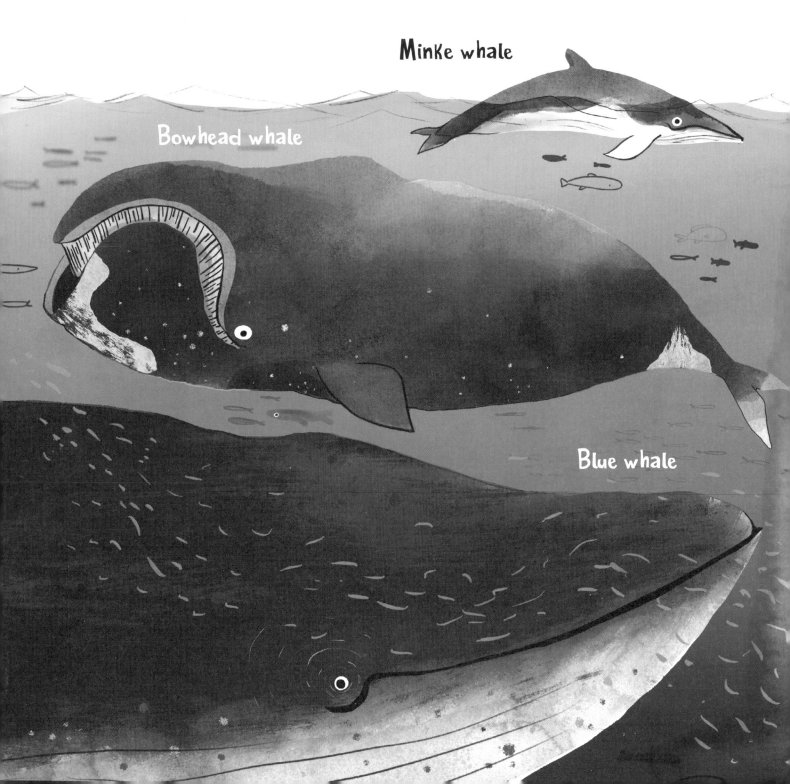

Minke whale

Bowhead whale

Blue whale